CAN YOU STILL SERVE
GOD
WITH AN UNCLEAN RECORD?

Rev. Jerome R. Milton

CAN YOU STILL SERVE
GOD
WITH AN UNCLEAN RECORD?

Rev. Jerome R. Milton

Goodwin Global
Publishing

**GOODWIN GLOBAL PUBLISHING, LLC
TYLER, TEXAS**

Copyright © 2023 by Rev. Jerome R. Milton
All rights reserved.
First Edition

Goodwin Global Publishing, LLC
Tyler, TX

Published by Goodwin Global Publishing, LLC 2023

Can You Still Serve God With An Unclean Record? may be purchased in
bulk for promotional, educational and business use through Goodwin
Global Publishing, LLC. Please fill out and submit contact form at
www.goodwinglobalpublishing.com for more information.

ISBN 979-8-9880975-0-1 (hardcover)
ISBN 979-8-9880975-1-8 (paperback)
ISBN 979-8-9880975-2-5 (digital)

Library of Congress Control Number: 2023910409

Cover designs by Renee Goodwin and Gabriela Fleming
Book design and layout by Gabriela Fleming

Printed in the United States of America

Dedications

My mom, Datie Florence Brown

– you believed in me when nobody else did.

– you always told me, "Rocky, don't let your abuse, be your excuse."

"The Catholic Nun"

– you inspired my years of success within the catholic school system.

CAN YOU STILL SERVE
GOD
WITH AN UNCLEAN RECORD?

Table of Contents

Preface

Having the best intentions within my ministry helping church members happenings unknown to me occurred and my positive intentions turned negative. Consequently, I served 180 days of incarceration. So now after fifty years in the ministry, forty years as a pastor and community leader it appears my clean record becomes unclean on paper (newspapers, television, social media).

But as I reflect in my writings, I can attest it is all by God's design. To further state, by the poser of God, I turned the jailhouse into God's House establishing the Whosoeverwill Church, bible study and daily prayer call at the county jail.

So, I ask, "Can you still serve God with an unclean record?" My answer, "Yes, I do and so can you!"

"My record is in heaven. My witness is on high!" (Job 16:19).

CHAPTER ONE

"You Can't Keep A Good Man Down"

Genesis 50:19-20

Y ou can't keep a good man down, when you walk with God. A prime example is found in the Old Testament story of Joseph, son of Jacob (Genesis Chapters 37-50). Joseph was his father's favorite son causing much jealousy among his brothers. Joseph's brothers conspired against him putting him DOWN in a pit. Then, Joseph found himself being thrown Down into prison. But, Joseph's God-given gifts raised him from the pit to the palace.

I know how Joseph must have felt being in prison for a frame-up and a set-up. Joseph made the best of his unfortunate situation and so did I. I was sentenced to six months in county jail. Similar to Joseph, I could have been oppressed, depressed, suppressed, stressed over, stressed out, stressed under. But I choose to make the best of it. When I was first put in jail, the inmates had many questions for me. Some knew me being a pastor, a coach, and a community leader. Others knew me from the news media over thirteen months of negative coverage. After several discussions within a few days, the inmates came to me asking to start a bible study class and hold church services. They shared that they grew up in church and wanted to become trained preachers and deacons. The class quickly grew to over fifteen students, held six days a week.

From there, I started the Whosoeverwill Church. Our first service had five attendees. The second service, twelve attended and the third service, nineteen attended. By the time we got to the fourth service, there were twenty-four in attendance out of forty-eight men in the pod.

As time passed, the daily bible study class grew, the Sunday church service grew to thirty-three to thirty-five men per Sunday. The multi-purpose room was filled to capacity. Unfortunately, a situation occurred causing the loss of the multi-purpose room privileges.

So, we started having bible study classes in the corner of the day room and our prayer call every night under the stairwell. For church service, it was suggested we go out to the recreation yard after lunch on Sundays. The men rallied each other so more would attend church service. Our first church service in the recreation yard was a huge success with thirty-eight men of forty-eight attending. The next Sunday, the men in a different pod viewing our church were adamant wanting to join. Special permission was granted allowing the two pods of inmates to meet in the recreation yard at the same time for church service. We had sixty plus inmates in church that day.

Such a happening had never ever, never ever taken place in the Smith County Jail. This monumental church service continued week after week becoming a life changing experience for many. During these church services, men were baptized, and memorial services were held for lost loved ones of the inmates. These memorial services gave closure to the men. The Whosoeverwill Church and bible classes met the needs of many.

Then, one night an officer told me to pack up. I was being moved to the Low-Risk Jail. The inmates were angry that I was being transferred. They cried as they hugged me and prayed for me. I stayed one night in the Low-Risk Jail and was transferred back to my pod. My transfer had been a mistake. But with that, God showed me the impact I had made for His glory. "You Can't Keep A Good Man Down."

The next day was the biggest celebration; a homecoming never seen before. But then, many of the original bible study students and the core church members began to be transferred to the Texas Department of Corrections. But the glory of God continues. It was time for the next generation of Whosoeverwill Church leaders. My cellmate, took the position of Timothy in the bible. He wanted to become a deacon. He asked me to teach him as Paul taught Timothy to spread the word of God. I taught and trained him every night. He became the assistant prayer call leader and church leader under me. Another young man became a church leader. Then, a young man with a beautiful voice became the song leader.

As many know in Tyler Smith County, I have been the organizer of the Martin Luther King (MLK) Day Parade and Celebration bringing diverse cultures together. I led this event for twenty-five years turning the leadership over to the Tyler Race Relations Forum. As it came to be, MLK Day that year occurred during my incarceration days. I wanted to have a march but my idea was put DOWN. I persisted and started the First Annual Smith County Jail MLK Day March. We marched around the recreation yard three times.

After my release, spending 180 days in the Smith County Jail, the prayer call continues and is going strong. I hope I led the men to believe, "You Can Still Serve God With An Unclean Record."

CHAPTER TWO

"Move To The Next Level"

Deuteronomy 5:1-7; Numbers 13:26-30

Moses was the greatest example of a man serving God with an unclean record. No prophet has risen again in Israel like Moses. There are multitudes of lessons we can learn, both good and bad. No matter what season of leadership we are currently in, here are eight things we can apply to our lives.

Number One: Leaders make mistakes, we should not run from them. In Exodus 2, we learn that Moses observed the oppression of his people. When an Egyptian struck one of the Israelites, Moses killed the Egyptian. Scared for his life, Moses fled to Midian and became a shepherd. God used this time to prepare Moses for his next assignment at the next level. You see friends, it is all by Godly design. "God doesn't call the equipped but He equips the called."

Number two: Moses faced opposition with

courage and confidence, not of himself but with the Lord. Not every leader will face an antagonist such as Pharoah, but every leader will face opposition. It would take several meetings with Pharoah before the Israelites were released from bondage. Two and a half million people, six hundred thousand families were freed. Moses led the people in the midst of opposition with courage but, God received the glory for the outcome.

Number three: Moses often interceded in prayer for the people even when they were difficult. Moses knew the power of teamwork. Moses learned this lesson from his father-in-law, Jethro when the work was too much for him to do alone. In Exodus 18: Jethro suggests to Moses that he delegate duties to other key leader allowing Moses to concentrate on major problems.

Number four: Moses through his examples to his leaders and his people (pleading with Pharaoh), you can still serve God with an unclean record.

Number five: Moses knew that the time had come for the people to move to the next level and go to the Promised Land. Israel had been delivered out of Egypt. Israel had camped out around Mount Horeb for about a year. Israel, because of their disobedience remained in the wilderness for 40 years. Israel would not move on to the next level. Moses wanted more for the Israelites than they wanted for themselves.

Number six: The Book of Numbers 13:26-30 reveals the sacred history of God's people wandering in the wilderness before entering the Promise Land. The Book of Numbers was written to demonstrate that God's plan for our lives will stay on track even when we get off track. The Book of Numbers shows how tolerant God was with the Israelites behavior. But know, God had a stopping point. The Book of Numbers shows that what God has for you is for you and what is for others is for them.

Number seven: We learn from this lesson that this is where you may be now but it is not where you have to stay. God is called El Shaddai, the God of More than Enough; not the God of barely enough; not the God of just enough; not the God of not enough. God is El Shaddai, the God of More than Enough.

We learn that it is not according to what you have but what God has. God owns it all. With one touch of God, favor can blast you out of barely enough and put you into more than enough. God can take you beyond your wildest dreams; beyond your family haters; beyond your church doubters; beyond your workplace "demotivators."

Often, we look at our circumstances and environments and think like the Israelites. We never get out of the wilderness mentally. We are out of "Egypt" but we can't get to the Promise Land because "Egypt" is not out of us. If you want something different, you have to do something different. If you want what you never had, you have to do what you have never done. If you keep viewing your obstacles as problems, you will never get out of your mental wilderness. You must view your problems as opportunities.

You can't stay like the Israelites. They saw their Giants as too tall; as too strong; as to mean for them. They saw the walls of Jericho as too high; too wide; too deep for them to conquer.

Number eight: Moses' challenging question to the children of Israel was, "What are you willing to settle for?" If you are to be God's chosen people, are you going to settle for the wilderness or the Promise Land? What was in the way of the Israelites going to the Promise Land? They thought they had to fight the Giants of the land so they decided it was better to settle in the wilderness.

My challenge to you: Don't settle for less than God's best for you! Ask yourself the question, "Why did I quit college, was the work too hard?" Life is hard. It takes hard work to get through the wilderness of life to reach the Promise Land. "Why did you quit your job, were people talking about me behind my back?" People don't talk about, plot against those that are not doing anything. People talk about, plot against, back stab others who are doing something, who want to be somebody, who don't want to stay in the wilderness but have the courage to go to the Promise Land.

Children of Israel had received a good report from the twelve spies viewing the Promise Land. Ten spies said it is true what God told Moses. In the Promise Land, there won't be houses to be built, nor roads to be made, nor gardens to be planted. The land was flowing with milk and honey. But the ten spies state, "We can't defeat the Giants in the land so we recommend settling in the wilderness."

After experiencing God leading the Israelites out of Egypt as a Pillar of Cloud by day and a Pillar of Fire by night, parting the Red Sea, feeding them manna (bread from heaven), giving them water from rocks, making quail fly low so they could have "rib-eye" quail, they would not trust God to fight their battle against the Giants. God never told the Israelites to fight the Giants. God just told them to go possess the land.

Moses, the servant of God with an unclean record was now leading a rebellious people with an unclean record! Moses dies on Mt. Nebo passing the baton to Joshua to lead the children of Israel, a new generation to the Promise Land. Joshua and Caleb believed God could defeat the Giants before them so they should not retreat to the wilderness.

Then Caleb quieted the people before Moses. Caleb said God had brought the Israelites this far. God would not leave them to settle in the wilderness. Caleb told the Israelites, "To move to the next level and possess the land." God has taught us through his servant Moses that we are able to possess the land. God has fought for us.

Moses sent twelve spies; Joshua sent only two spies. All takes place during three days when Joshua commands the people to wait on the banks of the Jordan. God has a special purpose for these three days. Joshua sent two spies from Acacia Grove, Caleb and the High Priest, Eliezer. Joshua shows wisdom by sending the two men secretly. Moses sent twelve spies publicly and the situation turned out bad for Israel when the majority of the spies returned with a discouraging report (Book of Numbers, Chapter 13). Joshua told the spies to view the land, especially Jericho.

The two spies came to Rahab's house, the house of a prostitute. We learn several lessons from this faith journey. First, don't be ashamed of the house when God is in the house. Rahab, who had an unclean record, received the two men of God gladly. The two spies had to hideout from the King's soldiers who were looking for them. The "Harlots House" became the place of grace for the two spies.

The next lesson we can learn is, "You never know who is going to have to cover you in the house." Rahab took the two men, covered them in the house and hid them. She risked her life for the sake of her family. Rahab confesses her faith in God (Joshua 2:8-14). Rahab, being a woman of faith yet with an unclean record still served God.

CHAPTER THREE

"It's Time to Change Your Clothes"

Zechariah 3:1-7

Zechariah tells a story of a vision he has about Joshua, a High Priest (Ezra 2:2). In his story, Zechariah questions indirectly, "What Do You Do When You Feel Useless and Unusable?" The bible shares stories of key people in the Old Testament; King David, Moses, Job, Joseph, Rahab, Elijah and in the New Testament; Apostle Peter, Apostle Paul, the Women at the Well, and Mary Magdalene that felt useless and unusable. There is no doubt we all can relate to feelings of uselessness and being unusable like these Old Testament and New Testament men and women of the bible.

In Zechariah's story of his vision, Joshua was well thought of in the community, and as a leader of the church. But Joshua sinned be it in the dark, on the front porch, on the back porch, in the closet or in the basement. Joshua sinned against God. As I read the story, in my sanctified imagination, I can visualize Joshua being on the front page of the Jerusalem Times, on all of the television networks, and featured in all of the magazines.

As Zechariah shares his vision, Joshua feels useless and unusable. Joshua has committed a sin and feels unworthy to continue to serve God with an unclean record. Everybody in town has turned against Joshua, his fellow prophets, his family, the church, the community. In the vision, Zechariah gets news that Satan has filed charges against Joshua stating Joshua has defiled the worship of God and he is due in court to stand before God.

Joshua had sinned and he questioned what he can do to defend himself. Joshua knows he is unclean to stand before God. Joshua was not worried about what Satan knew about him. Joshua was worried about what God knew about him. Joshua was visually filthy wearing dirty robes and a dirty headdress. Joshua is ashamed of himself, ashamed to be in the church, ashamed to be the High Priest.

In the vision, Jesus, the angel of the Lord is in the court room. But Jesus is silent in his defense of

Joshua because Satan's accusations against Joshua were true and his clothes were filthy. He was totally unprepared for court, and totally unpresentable to see God. As a High Priest, he knew he was no longer fit to serve.

Have you been where Joshua is or do you know someone who has shared Joshua's plight? What Joshua could not say in his own defense, the angel of the Lord could. In the vision, Jesus stopped being the prosecuting attorney and became Joshua's defense attorney. This is what Jesus did for us at the cross. He looked beyond our faults and saw our needs realizing that all have sinned and come short of the glory of God (Romans 3:23). But God demonstrates His own love for us in this: While we were still sinners, Christ died for us. (Romans 5:8). For God so loved the world that He gave His one and only Son, that whosoever believes in him should not perish but have eternal life (John 3:16).

Satan wants to make sure Joshua never gets motivated to want to come back, get on track. So, what do you do when Satan turns up the heat? God will rescue you from your fire and pull your stick out of the fire of trials, tribulations, and troubles. God will leave your stick in the fire long enough for you to feel the heat. God will leave you in the fire to refine you. God does not want to destroy you but to develop you. God will allow you to go through some satanic fire storms in life so you won't become your own worst enemy. God will save you no matter how high Satan turns up the heat. With God's grace and mercy, you can beat the heat.

God will pull your stick out of the fire and you won't look like what you have been through. I am reminded of the three Hebrew boys, Shadrach, Meshach and Abednego that King Nebuchadnezzar had in the fiery furnace (Daniel 3). The furnace was turned up seven times hotter than ever before. The next morning, the three Hebrew boys walked out of the fiery furnace. Jesus helped them beat the heat. Jesus will help us beat the heat. God will barbecue your haters, and your "demotivators," and put love sauce on them, forgiveness sauce on them, another chance sauce on them so you can always smell them when they are coming.

In the vision, the question is asked, "What do you do when you are not presentable to meet the judge?" Jesus had those priests that were in the temple to take off the old filthy clothes and bring some new clothes. This reminds me of the parable of the Prodigal Son when the son came home, the father ran to meet him on the road. The son had dirty, filthy clothes. The son was dirty, filthy. The son smelled like the hog pen. But the father had the servants take off the son's dirty clothes and put on a new robe, a new ring, and new shoes. The father forgave his son, restored his son, revived his son, renewed his son (Luke 15:11-31).

In the vision, God being the judge, forgave Joshua. Joshua was given clean clothes. The clothes made him presentable. The turbine made him acceptable. The angel of the Lord made him usable again. God reminded Satan, I chose Joshua. Joshua didn't choose me. Joshua is now made presentable to meet the judge. God restored Joshua back to his high priestly office on the condition that he would walk in His ways, and keep His charge. God will restore you to judge His house and keep the courts of His house. And, you will walk tall, with your head up and shoulders back among everybody in God's house that is standing by.

Now remember, when God forgives you don't run and hide. When God is on your side, get up, get out, get going in the ministry that he has restored you to. Don't shame God by hanging your head down. Bless God by lifting your head up and raising up above all your storms and midnight problems. I can testify. Don't make God regret He gave you another chance to do bigger, greater things in ministry. You can still serve God with an unclean record.

What we find out in Zechariah 3:1-7 is that you can still serve God with an unclean record in spite of all of your faults and defaults. Jesus still uses his "usable" servants in spite of all of your dirt and filth. Jesus still forgives the "unforgivable" servants. In spite of all of your mistakes, Jesus still loves the "unlovable". You know when your past is closed, you don't reopen wounds God has closed. You don't reopen doors God has closed. You don't reopen windows God has closed.

You can still serve God with an unclean record. Jesus' blood cleans and clears the slate for a new day, a new beginning, a new way, a fresh start, a greater start, a better start.

CHAPTER FOUR

"With Friends Like These"

Job 42:12-17

In Job, Chapters 1 and 2, God calls a heavenly business meeting where the sons of God (the heavenly angels) are giving their reports of their stewardships to God. Satan is also present and God asks for Satan's report, too. Satan replies that he is going in and out, up and down seeking who he can destroy. God asked Satan if he had considered His servant, Job, saying "There is no one on earth like him" (Job 1:8).

Satan questioned if Job would serve God for nothing. Satan says to God that God has blessed Job's hand and has a hedge around him. Satan bargains telling God if You lower the hedge You have around Job and let me put forth my hand against him, I will make him curse You to your face. God says to Satan that all Job has is now in Satan's hands (Job 1:9-12).

Job had seven sons, three daughters 7000 sheep, 3000 camels, 500 yoke of oxen, and 500 mules. Job was the greatest in the East. Four servants came to Job at separate times to tell him the bad news that his children, his houses, his land, his livestock had all been killed or destroyed. After this, Job shaved his head and fell down on the ground and worshiped God saying, "Naked I came from my mother's womb, and naked I will depart. The Lord gave and the Lord has taken away; may the name of the Lord be praised" (Job 1:21).

After this, in Chapter 2, Satan gives his report to God and asks God for another chance, skin for skin, if God would let Satan touch Job, then Satan would make Job curse God to His face. God granted Satan his request with the condition that Satan not touch Job's soul and Satan agreed. Friends, this was a bad deal for Satan. Man is a trichotomy; body, soul and spirit. God was saying that Satan could touch the dirt man comes from but not the soul and spirit, the breath of life God breathes into man. In other words, Satan could not touch God.

Job's wife wants Job to curse God and die. She is looking at her husband who all of his life was strong, vibrant, respected in the church community and among his children. She could not take Job's suffering anymore and says to Job who she loves with all of her heart to end this hurting, just curse God and die.

What many people fail to realize in this biblical drama is that Job is not the only one that lost children and houses and land. Job's wife lost children, houses, land and livestock. Job responded to his loving wife saying she spoke like one of the foolish women. Job did not call his wife a fool. He just said she was sounding like a fool.

Job feels like he is dying. Job 14:14, "If someone dies shall they live again? All the days of my hard service I will wait for my renewal to come." Job's friends, Eliphaz, Bildad and Zophar come to visit him. They are trying to get Job to repent. Job's friends believed you can't serve God with an unclean record. They believed that Job had a secret sin that God was cursing Job for. For nine months, Job was trying to serve God with what looked like an unclean record.

I can feel for Job. I have been in ministry for fifty years. I was a pastor for forty years, an award-winning track and field coach winning ten state championships. I was the first Afro-American in Tyler Smith County, Texas to win the prestigious T.B. Butler Citizen of the Year award. I was featured in Sports Illustrated Magazine as an Outstanding Coach. I was pastor of the week and gave the invocation to the U.S. House of Representatives. I was a church pastor for thirty-two years where I remodeled the church with an elevator, established the Wall of Honor recognizing outstanding church members, built a prayer room, church annex, youth center, children's playground, and a prayer garden. I had the street behind the church named the "Ioatie Flowers Street," who at the time of writing this book is 105 years old. I built the Datie Florence Brown Children's Home and the Dunbar Reading Academy helping mothers with young children that needed assistance.

I helped many members get jobs and houses. I helped many families get their children out of trouble by appearing on their behalf in court. I organized the building of the Billy E. Hibbs, Sr. Memorial Football Field for disadvantaged youth in Tyler, Texas. I help many students go to college on scholarships. As an athletic scholarship coordinator, I sent over two hundred students to colleges and universities on athletic scholarships.

Although many leaders of different cultures made it an uphill battle, I started the annual M.L. King, Jr. March and community wide celebration in 1990 and the Youth March in 1995. The rest is history as these marches and celebrations continue today.

I worked hard in our Baptist Organization, local, state and national levels, as State President of our Sunday School Convention and special assistant to the National Sunday School President. I placed over seventy of our pastors, men and women in positions of importance. Never in the history of our convention had so many from one area of the county been assigned.

Yet, after all of this, after all of this, I spent 180 days incarcerated. I know how Job felt when Eliphaz, Bildad and Zophar accused him of having secret sins and God was punishing him.

Like Job, I felt betrayed, denied, unappreciated by so many that I had sacrificed so much for. During my time in Smith County Jail, I thought of Job's nine-month nightmare often. But, the story and faithfulness of this Great Servant of God helped me persevere.

Job is so depressed, so empty. He wants to know where God is, where has God been, if God is coming to heal him, save him, restore him, revive him, renew him. After this, God shows up in a whirlwind. God said to Job, "Who is this that obscures my plans with words without knowledge?" (Job 38:2). In Job 42:2, Job answers God, "I know that you can do all things; no purpose of yours can be thwarted." Job realized his plight as I realized my plight was all by God's design.

Job 42:7 states, "After the Lord had said these things to Job, He said to Eliphaz the Temanite, I am angry with you and your two friends, because you have not spoken the truth about me, as my servant Job has." God had Eliphaz, Bildad and Zophar take a burnt offering to Job so that Job could pray for them. Job prayed for his "Frienimies" and forgave their meanness, betrayal, put downs, shut downs, and cut downs of him.

If Job had not prayed for them, if Job had not forgiven them, God would have cursed them. Job showed kindness and God gave Job "double for all of his trouble."

Put yourself in Job's place. Could you do it? Could you forgive your family that walked out on you? Could you forgive the church that turned their backs on you? Could you forgive all of your close friends that talked about you and lied about you? All the time knowing if you don't pray for them and forgive them, God is going to deal with them in a bad way.

Could you do it as you think about your bruises, wounds, hurts and scars? Could you do it when you think about what they could have done for you, your family to get you through to the other side of through? Remember, Jesus on the cross says, "Father, forgive them for they do not know what they are doing" (Luke 23:34).

Job lived one hundred and forty years more. Job saw his sons and their sons grow-up. Job showed, you can serve God with an unclean record.

CHAPTER FIVE

"Sometimes You Have to Lose to Win"

2 Samuel 19:1-8

If there is anybody that knows how you feel when everybody has turned against you, it is King David. King David has gone from the highest of highs to the lowest of lows. The people that King David was leading were like many of us today. We can identify with the pain but not the lesson of the pain.

It is easy to lose your passion when you've been hurt by peers on the job, wounded by church members, bruised by family and relatives. It is easy to lose your passion when in your darkest hour, friends now become "Frienimies." It is easy to lose your passion when everybody is high-fiving you one day and low-fiving you the next day.

In Jesus' triumphant entry into Jerusalem, the people were waving palms one day, shouting hosanna one day, putting their coats on the ground one day, putting their coats on the donkey one day but then cried, "Crucify Him" a few days later.

King David had to learn to stop thinking about who was against him and concentrate on who was for him. King David had an encounter with his closest friend and ally Joab. Absolom, King David's son had turned against him. Absolom got almost all of the men of the kingdom turned against King David. King David had to flee for his life and the life of his family, going from cave to cave, forest to forest.

But Joab killed Absolom, King David's son who had betrayed him. The people that sacrificed and stayed with King David through thick and thin shouted and praised God. But King David their leader was absent from the celebration. The people were concerned about their king and they went to Joab, David's best friend to see what was wrong with King David. The people wanted to know why King David was absent from the celebration.

Joab knew where King David was. Joab knew King David was hiding far back into the caves. Joab finds King David unkept, hair uncombed, beard not cut, clothes dirty, robe filthy. Joab could hear David mourning over Absolom, crying out, "O my son

Absolom! O Absolom, my son, my son!" (2 Samuel 19:4).

Joab counseled King David asking do you think Absolom would be crying over you? What if I was killed, would you be crying over me? We are the ones who have sacrificed our lives for you, our wives and children for you. You hate who you should love and love who you should hate. Clean yourself up and lead us back to Jerusalem. Take your rightful place on the throne. Because if you don't, we will never follow you again. We will never call your name again. And the God we serve will put worse things upon you (2 Samuel 19:5-7).

Through his suffering, David learned to be a better leader, a better King. King David learned he could serve God with an unclean record. If God brings you to it, God will see you through it. King David had to go through a journey to one day live up to the title of being king.

In our lives, we must go through our own journey of life to earn the title champion, president, director, supervisor, coordinator, pastor. King David went through some inconvenient detours in reaching his anointed destiny. Don't tell me what you have been through, tell me what you have come through. If God brings you to it, God will bring you through it.

King David had to learn that God does not always make sense. King David had to learn he couldn't take everybody with him on his journey. King David had to learn that everybody that lives in your "now" can't always live in your "future." King David had to learn he could not always call "Heaven 911" and rescue everybody, especially when they were calling "Hell 666" to destroy him. God does not always make sense but God gives you sense to have common sense.

King David had to learn the difference between the right place versus the right time. Sometimes in life, it can be the right place but the wrong time; right time but the wrong place; right people in the wrong place; right place with the wrong people. It is all by design. God is shaping you for the right place, the right time with the right people.

King David learned he had to encourage himself. Many of our family and friends want what you can do for them but they don't want you. People wanted what Jesus could do for them. They wanted his bread, fish, wine, healing, miracles but they did not want Jesus.

God once said that King David was a man after His own heart because King David was different than Adam. Adam blamed God and Eve for everything. King David blamed himself (Psalm 51:1-13). Despite his trespasses against God, God still used King David in his ministry. King David is a shining example of how God uses men with unclean records.

If you are reading this book and you have fallen from grace in your ministry of life, please know you can still serve God with an unclean record like King David. God will restore you, revive you, renew you. God will put your ministry, your life under new management. God will make you His new and improved servant. God will give you a new start, a new beginning, a new outlook on your life and ministry. God will empower unexpected people to be in unexpected places, to do unexpected things to inspire you on your unexpected journey. Therefore, with God, always expect the unexpected!

CHAPTER SIX

"You Have To Let It Go"

Isaiah 6:1-6

Many times, things block our vision of God. We feel secure in our job. We feel secure in our home. We feel secure in our leaders. We know God, we love God, we trust God but yet are we really depending on Him?

Many times, God will remove our safety nets. We become ill, we lose our job, our leader dies, we go to jail, we go to prison. We ask ourselves the questions, "What are we going to do now? How will we survive?"

The throne is now empty. Uzziah had held things together. What will happen to us now, Ephraim and Syria are threating to invade us. When we look at Isaiah; Devastation – personal tragedy; King Uzziah is dead. Aggravation – political tragedy; someone has to step up and lead and Isaiah knows it can't be

him because he has an unclean record. Frustration –
professional tragedy; Isaiah was not prepared to lead
because he was unclean and the people were unclean.

Isaiah looks to God for some directive. Isaiah
looked to God for an answer and God gave the
prophet Isaiah a vision. God was sitting on the
throne. The throne was empty. God has things in
control. God was going to look beyond Isaiah's faults
and see his needs. God was going to look beyond
Isaiah's dirt and see the gold in his life even if Isaiah
thought he was useless and unusable. God was going
to look beyond the darkness of Isaiah's life and save
the light of his life in ministry.

In the vision, God wanted the prophet Isaiah
to be restored, revived, renewed to a greater sense
of purpose. Sometimes from your greatest rejection
in life you will find your greatest directions in life.
Sometimes from your deepest hurts, bruises, and
wounds you will find your deepest strength to carry-
on.

In the vision, Isaiah saw something that happened
at the church house that did not happen at his house.
When you go to the house of the Lord, something
should happen to you and your loved ones that can't

happen anywhere else but church. You should hear something, feel something, do something, be a part of something that can't happen anywhere else but in God's church. Like Isaiah, you need to be mesmerized by God's majesty.

Isaiah thought he could not serve God with an unclean record. But the spirit of God will raise you above all of your haters, your naysayers. The higher you rise above something, the smaller it becomes.

Isaiah realized he had to thank God for his haters and use them as his motivators and elevators to move significantly higher as a leader and serve as a prophet of God. Isaiah was also enthralled by God's ability to take uncleanliness and make it spotless.

I tell my family, my church, and the community I started from below nothing so when I got to the level of nothing, I thought I had something. I also tell my haters, doubters, and "demotivators" don't hate on my glory until you know my story. I was born in San Diego, California. I was raised in the foster care system for 18 years; 14 foster homes and an orphanage where we were fed cat food, dog food, and grossly abused. The orphanage affiliates could get away with it because we had no names on our birth certificates identifying us.

A Catholic nun finally got me out of the orphanage and after 13 foster homes I was placed with a lady from Wynn, Arkansas who taught me not to let my abuse be my excuse. She led me to Jesus and inspired me to go on and play college football at UCLA, to run track and field and participate in the Olympic trials. All she wanted me to do for her was to do for other foster children what she had done for me and forty-four other foster children. In fulfilling my promise to her, my wife and I have adopted six children from Child Protective Services of the State of Texas.

The Catholic nun asked me to do the same thing; to do for a group of children what she had done for me. In thanksgiving for what the Catholic nun did for me, I worked for thirty years in a catholic school system serving as a scholarship coordinator placing over two hundred academic athletes on scholarships in colleges and universities.

Isaiah still feels so unworthy as I felt unworthy coming from where I came from. In Isaiah's vision, a seraphim angel dispatched from the throne of God brought a tong from the alter and touched the lips of

Isaiah with it. The seraphim angel proclaimed Isaiah's iniquity was taken away. His sin was now purged.

God will remove all obstacles that are in your way, including you, that get in the way of God's designed purpose for your life and ministry. Now Isaiah knows he can serve God with an unclean record. Now, Isaiah could hear the call of God. Who can we send for us? Who will go for us? Isaiah can now answer, "Here I am, send me."

I am asked over and over again, "Pastor Milton, can I still serve God with an unclean record? They tell me, "I want to serve God even though I have an unclean record but, so many people cut me down, put me down, and shove me down." I say to you and everyone that feels this way, "You have to let it go." Let the wounds go, let the bruises go. Let the hurts go, let the anger go. Let the resentment go, let them go, let them go, let them go. Let those church people go, let those street people go. Let those family members go, let those work people go. It is time for you to change the channel and serve God with an unclean record for His glory and honor. Amen.

CHAPTER SEVEN

"What Do You Do When Everything Is All Dried Up?"

I Kings 17:1-16, 19:1-18

Are you ready for the next season of your ministry? Are you ready for the next season of your professional career? Are you ready to be restored, renewed and revived? Are you ready for God, the Holy Spirit to refresh you with favor so that your life and ministry will no longer be dried up?

For this cause, Elijah was sent by God to the brook named Cherith to retool his ministry, preaching, teaching and healing. For this cause, God will take you on an emotional, mental and spiritual sabbatical. Let me be very transparent here. God sent me on a spiritual sabbatical in Smith County, Texas jail for six months. I was able to preach to the least of these men in orange jumpsuits. I was able to show them God cares for the utmost to the "gutter most." God saves us as is and cleans us as is so we can serve Him as is.

God put me in Smith County Jail by design so I could be his pastor to the men in orange. God brought me from where I was after fifty years in the ministry, forty years as a pastor to pastor The Whosoeverwill Church. For six months many men were truly saved, truly called to preach, truly called to be deacons. This was not a jailhouse religion. Many received the blessings and graces of God as they were baptized within The Whosoeverwill Church.

We had prayer call every night. We had bible study for two hours a day, six days a week. Church service in the recreation yard on Sunday for thirty minutes. Many of the guards and nurses joined in the Church services. We had memorial services for our brothers who lost loved ones, simulating the grave yard services they missed. I look forward to seeing many of those men in my church service at Open Door Bible Church in the days to come.

Elijah had just accomplished a mountain top experience defeating eight hundred prophets of Baal and four hundred prophets of Grove. Elijah goes to King Ahab by God's design and tells King Ahab, "As the Lord the God of Israel, lives, whom I serve, there shall be neither dew, nor rain in the next three years except at my word." (I Kings 17:1). In other words, everything is going to be all dried-up. God tells Elijah, "Leave here, turn eastward and hide in the Kerith Ravine, east of the Jordan. You will drink from the brook, and I have directed the ravens to supply you with food there." (I Kings 17:2-4). So, the ravens brought Elijah bread in the morning and "rib-eye" quail at night.

King Ahab told his Queen (Jezebel) what had happened. Queen Jezebel had a demonic spirit on her, so big, so evil, so powerful. Elijah was not afraid of Queen Jezebel, herself. Elijah was afraid of what was on Queen Jezebel, the demonic spirit. Elijah ran.

Jezebel was a self-styed and self-styled appointed prophetess and priestess. But just because you call yourself something does not mean you are that something. This is why Jezebel hated Elijah. Elijah was willing to serve God no matter what even with an unclean record. Elijah, the fearless prophet of God instead of running to the problem like many of us, he ran away from the problem.

I often wonder why Elijah ran. He called down fire from heaven. He didn't even consult God. He had that much faith in God and his relationship with

God that God would be God on Mount Carmel. Again, it was not Queen Jezebel of the Old Testament that he was frightened of. It was the demonic spirit Jezebel that Elijah was afraid of. Oh, my friend, the demonic spirits of Jezebel are still alive and well in the church today. The demonic spirit of Jezebel is still attacking God's pastors, preachers, deacons, ministry leaders and that is why our churches, our ministries, our church conferences and conventions are all dried up.

As I mentioned earlier, Elijah was taken care of by the ravens and not the doves or the eagles. Sometimes God will allow the dirty birds of our lives to take care of us in the dark times, dangerous times and the dirty times. Elijah was taken care of by the ravens. Elijah's every need was met by the ravens. Elijah was depressed, oppressed, suppressed, discouraged, disgusted, disappointed but he was encouraged by the ravens every morning and every night.

Elijah is wrestling with himself. Can he still serve God with an unclean record? When Elijah arrived at Mount Horeb, God asked him why had he chosen such a remote place to hide. Elijah responded to God that Israel had rejected His covenant. Israel had torn down His alters and put His prophets to death. Elijah told God he was the only one left and now they were trying to kill him, too (I Kings 19:10).

Elijah saw himself as the lone defender of the faith and it appeared to Elijah that the demonic spirit of Jezebel was winning the fight. But God let Elijah know that He had seven thousand servants that never bowed their knees to Baal (I Kings 19:18). We learn that just because we don't see them doesn't mean God does not have them.

God was now ready for Elijah to move to the next level of his ministry. When God gets ready to move you to the new level, new place, new destiny, new journey, new place of grace, sometimes God has to dry your brook up. We can get comfortable with our ravens feeding us, taking care of us, protecting us that we will never be who or what God wants us to be.

My mom told me those many years ago with tears in her eyes, "Rocky, God has placed on my heart to tell you, for you to move to the next level in his ministry, you are going to have to leave California." I followed my mother's advice and the spirit of God and came to East Texas. I have been very successful as a senior pastor, track and field coach and community leader. Just like Elijah, I didn't allow my brook to dry up.

Elijah leaves a dried-up cave, a dried-up brook, and goes to a dried-up place called Zarephath. God told Elijah when he got to Zarephath he would find a widowed woman there that would assist him. Many of you are praying to Go to do something about your dried-up churches, dried-up homes, dried-up jobs, dried-up marriages, dried-up relationships. Maybe your brook is still dried-up because you have turned your nose up at the ravens and the widows.

Elijah arrives in Zarephath and finds a widow woman picking dried-up sticks with a dried-up pot, dried-up plates, dried-up table. She was preparing her final meal for her and her sons to then die in a dried-up house. In other words, the prophet Elijah found everything all dried-up. As the widow woman takes the last morsel of bread to feed her and her sons as they prepare to die, Elijah tells the widow to serve him first (I Kings 17:7-16). Elijah's request to feed him first is strange, sounding rather selfish. Sometimes God doesn't make sense but God always, as shown in the bible, works in mysterious ways, making a way out of no way and making sense out of nonsense all the time.

The faith of this widow woman is to be admired. I believe God had her mind and heart prepared for Elijah. Elijah's journey was all by God's design. God has a purpose and cause for your life and ministry. It is all by design to show the world that you can still serve God with an unclean record.

CHAPTER EIGHT

"Don't Let Your Situation Get the Best of You"

John 13:37-38; 21:15-17

Luke 22:32-33

I want to encourage all of you on my way to heaven on a 747 Cloud with a first-class ticket to heaven purchased by the blood of Jesus Christ our Lord and Savior, if you have been wounded, shattered, battered, tattered and bruised, don't let your situation get the best of you. Jesus can still give you a clean record and make you whole again.

In our scripture, Jesus is having a pep talk with Peter and Jesus gives Peter a glimpse of a situation that is going to happen in the future. Jesus shares with Peter because Jesus didn't want Peter to throw in the towel. As many of you can recall, Peter asked Jesus, "Lord, why can't I follow you now? I will lay down my life for you." Then Jesus answered, "Will you really lay down your life for me? Very truly I tell you, before the rooster crows, you will disown me three times." (John 13:37-38).

Peter felt useless and unusable. Peter wanted to throw in the towel on his ministry, throw in the towel on his faith, throw in the towel on his calling as an Apostle. How many of you today have felt like Peter? You have disappointed yourself, disappointed your family, disappointed your church. And you feel like you are good for nothing in ministry, good for nothing in the church, good for nothing in the community, good for nothing in the family.

Jesus wanted Peter to know in spite of all of his faults, in spite of all of his dirt, in spite of all of his denials, in spite of all of his betrayals that he was going to look beyond the dirt and see the gold in his life and ministry. Jesus wanted Peter to know that Peter could still serve God with an unclean record. Jesus said to Simon Peter, "Simon son of John, do you love me more than these?" Yes, Lord," he said, "you know that I love you." Jesus said, "Feed my lambs." (John 21:15-17). Jesus will look beyond your faults and your dirt and see the gold in your life and ministry.

Sometimes in life, no matter how well intended, you will make some mistakes, some misjudgments that will be misunderstood by social media, print media, television media. But sometimes God will allow these unfortunate events to happen in your life. No, God does not condone any wrong doing by any of his believers but, sometimes you are chosen to be an encouragement to so many others that you can still serve God with an unclean record.

In my own life and ministry, after fifty years in ministry, forty years as a pastor, a clean record in the church, a clean record in the community, a clean record as an educator, a clean record in my church conference, the devil stained my record, but it was all by God's design. I spent six months in Smith County Jail in Tyler, Texas. But by doing so, God allowed me to form The Whosoeverwill Church for His glory and honor.

My friends, I must admit to you, God had so prepared my spirit, soul, heart, mind that I immediately was ready to do His will. I was not ashamed of the Gospel of Christ. I was not ashamed of being a pastor. I was not ashamed to call those men in orange my brothers and my friends. I was not ashamed to preach to them, teach them, reach them, pastor them because for this cause and this design, God allowed me to be sentenced to six months in county jail.

I want to encourage all of you that are incarcerated, jailed or imprisoned, God will look beyond your faults, your dirt, your conviction and use you with an unclean record for His glory and His honor. My head is held up, my shoulders are back. Thank God I am back on track. God can still use me with an unclean record.

Jesus wanted to paint a picture in Peter's mind about the devil's agenda; it is hard to get hit by a train if you know it is coming. "Simon, Simon, Satan has asked to sift all of you as wheat. But I have prayed for you, Simon, that your faith may not fail." (Luke 22:31-32).

It is important to understand that the devil wants to get his hands on you, on Peter, to expose faults, short-comings, weaknesses and sins. For the purpose of discrediting your testimony, your legacy, the devil figures if he can get you, get Peter, then the devil can get the rest of us or make all of us so frightened that all will run away from Peter, from Jesus, the church and their ministries.

I want to further encourage you, if your situation has you in broken pieces, I know a Savior who specializes in mending broken lives, broken men, broken women, broken homes, broken churches into masterpieces. Well, not only did Jesus give Peter a portrait of the devil's future agenda for his life and ministry but the text also reveals Jesus prayed for Peter. Jesus is going from his prophetic role on earth to his high priestly role in heaven on the right hand of God as he prays for Peter.

I am happy to report to you that Jesus is praying for you and me and our ministries especially when our name comes up like Job. In other words, when you are doing good for God, you start catching hell from everywhere. Your name and ministry just came up at the business meeting in heaven. The devil is telling God, let me tout his name in the newspaper, let me trash his name on the news for over a year, let me trash and bash his name on the radio and in the churches. I know this pastor who has served you for fifty years will turn his back on you, the church, family and hate the day You ever called him to ministry.

But like my friend, Apostle Peter, in spite of all I have been through, God has brought me to the other side of through. Thank God by His grace, I don't look like what I have been through.

But thank God for a few friends, a few lawyers, a few pastors, a few community leaders, a few former athletes, a few parents, a few family members. Oh, thank God for just a few. This is why I can serve God with an unclean record.

Jesus does not want to see us down and out, broken and hurt, wounded and distraught when our situation starts to get the best of us. Jesus wants us blessed not stressed, healed not sick, up not down. Jesus did not want Peter's situation to get the best of him, his denial warming himself by the enemy fire, his betrayal. Jesus prayed for Peter (Luke 22: 32).

Jesus is praying for us that when the dust settles down, and the rain drops of trouble stop falling and the storm cease and the chilly winds of adversity stop blowing in your life, we still will be able to serve God with an unclean record. Lastly and finally, Jesus not only gives Peter a portrait of the devil's agenda, a prayer of the high priest. But Jesus reveals to Peter the purpose of his pain. We all have asked God the question, "Why me, Lord?"

Jesus says to Peter, "When you have turned back, strengthen the brothers." (Luke 22:32). Jesus guides Peter to return and receive the word. Strengthen means to make stable, to make firm. Peter finds out from Jesus that his trouble, trials, tribulations are all by design. Peter had to learn to lead and bleed while serving God with an unclean record.

CHAPTER NINE

"Leave Your Water Pots Behind"

John 4:5-42

In John Chapter 3, Jesus has a conversation with a man named Nicodemus. Nicodemus was religious. Nicodemus was moral. Nicodemus was well-known. Nicodemus was well-liked. In John Chapter 4, Jesus has a conversation with a nameless woman at the well. In the bible, this is the longest recorded conversation that Jesus has with any one person. The woman was a sinner. The woman was classless. The woman was also well-known but, in a negative sense.

The woman at the well did not understand why a Jewish man in the middle of the day would be talking with a Samaritan woman knowing full well that they had no dealing with each other. Jesus asked her for some water. The Samaritan woman said to him, "You are a Jew and I am a Samaritan woman. How can you ask me for a drink?" Jesus answers her, "If you knew the gift of God and who it is that asks you for a drink, you would have asked him and he would have given you living water." "Sir", the woman said, "you have nothing to draw with and the well is deep. Where can you get this living water?" (John 4:11). The woman said to him, "Sir, give me this water so that I won't get thirsty and have to keep coming here to draw water (John 4:15).

Jesus told her, "Go, call your husband and come back. "I have no husband, she replied." Jesus said to her, "You are right when you say you have no husband. The fact is, you have had five husbands, and the man you now have is not your husband. What you have just said is quite true." "Sir," the woman said, "I can see you are a prophet." (John 4:16-19). The woman from this point moves from being a mistress to being a missionary. She becomes a missionary with an unclean record.

She left her water pots and went back to her hometown of Sychar and told the men to come see a man that told her everything that she ever did posing the question, "Is this not the Christ? You can imagine that the men were very concerned thinking that this man the woman spoke of may be the Christ, the promised Messiah. But, at the same time, they were concerned about their unclean records since possibly they may have previously had a relationship with the woman.

Every now and then we have to leave our water pots behind and serve God even with unclean records. What are our water pots; water pots of shame, water pots of guilt, water pots of criticism, ostracism, and being minimized? We have to leave our water pots that are obstacles to us serving God even with unclean records.

I am impressed with her because the woman at the well went back to her hometown where everybody knew her record. The men of the church and the community that should have been lifting her up in the Lord were letting her down to the devil. The women in the church that should have been praying with her were preying on her with their white dresses and black hearts.

It is time to drop your water pots. You have to drop bad habits, bad people, bad memories of the past. You can't live in the past and the present at the same time. If you want something different, you have to do something different. If you want what you never had, you have to do what you have never done before.

Why did the woman at the well go back to her hometown? Because there were so many like her that believed they could no longer serve God with an unclean record. She wanted them to know a man that said you can serve God with an unclean record. Therefore, it is time to leave your water pots at the well and serve God with unclean records.

CHAPTER TEN

"I Am What I Am"

I Cor 15: 9-10

Paul was being criticized by the Jews for being a lesser apostle than the other eleven apostles. Paul whose name was Saul was a great persecutor of the church. One day while Paul was traveling to Damascus to destroy the church, Jesus knocked him off of his horse midway between Damascus and Jerusalem. Paul fell to the ground and heard a voice say to him, "Saul, Saul, why do you persecute me?" (Acts 9:4).

Jesus is calling to the apostolic ministry a man who hated God, who hated the church, who hated pastors of the church. Jesus is taking a man with an unclean record to pastor people with unclean records. Like the apostle Paul, you don't have to come from a family of saints, preachers, choir directors in order for God to do "great things through you."

The people of Corinth did not like Paul. They thought he was a fraud and did not believe that the God they served would call such a man as Paul to be an apostle. Paul's defense to the church of Corinth was the truth. Paul let them know everything they heard about him was true; he did burn down the churches, he did kill the pastors, he did drag the church members into court and had them put into prison.

But whether you believe me or not I have seen the resurrected Christ. Paul lets the church at Corinth know that "by the grace of God, I am what I am" (I Cor. 15: 10). Paul tells Corinth that his record is unclean, his reputation is unclean but God has picked him up, set him up, cleaned him up and God is going to use him up with an unclean record.

As many of you know the Apostle Paul wrote the great majority of the New Testament. If there is anybody in the bible that absolutely should not be a preacher, pastor, bible teacher, it is the Apostle Paul. But, for Christ, Paul lived and for Christ, Paul died.

How many bad boys and girls have you grown up with in church that later in life, God called them to be pastors, preachers, evangelist, and missionaries.

They thought they were useless and unusable but God still used them with unclean records. So many have come up to me and asked the question, "Pastor Milton, how can you serve God with an unclean record and everybody in town knows your record, they know your faults, your basement sins, closet sins, backyard sins." And I answer them by saying, "Look at Apostle Paul. He told the church at Corinth, he was not what people said he was. Paul told the people that he was what Jesus said he was." In other words, nothing spoken about you has to define who you are. People can call you a lot of things but you are only what you call yourself that is why Paul said, "by the grace of God, I am what I am." (I Cor. 15:10).

Even when Jesus went to his hometown of Nazareth, they did not believe that anyone from their hometown could be great, do great things or have a great position because no one from Nazareth had ever done anything great. Now you are telling me that the carpenter's son is the promised Messiah, "Ya Right."

How many times have people said that about your family or your hometown? Well, it is time to prove them wrong. It is time for you to blaze new trails, trod new pathways, reach new stars, claim new mountains. No matter your past, God can, God will, God has used people with unclean records. For His glory and His honor, I am a living witness. God will use you with an unclean record.

EPILOGUE

In conclusion, after reading these divinely guided words upon these pages and now answering the question, Can you still serve God with an unclean record?, I pray you know the answer is "Yes!" No matter what our backgrounds, our foregrounds or our in-betweens, we are all sinners, living our daily imperfect lives with our eyes on our perfect Jesus. Jesus, is all merciful. Jesus shed his blood for the forgiveness of our sins bringing us eternal life.

ACKNOWLEDGMENTS

For the devotion of my wife Charlene, adopting and raising our children with me.

For the loyalty of family members, special friends, pastors, lawyers, former student-athletes, and parents.

For the commitment of community leaders, the Tyler Ministerial Alliance, Tyler, Texas.

For the forever dedication of the church members of the Open Door Bible Fellowship Church.

For those who honored me as a pastor and a church leader becoming members of The Whosoeverwill Church, Smith County Jail, Tyler, Texas.

The chaplains of the Smith County Jail, Tyler, Texas, for your devotions to the ministry.

ABOUT THE AUTHOR

Rev. Jerome R. Milton is a minister, pastor, coach and first-time author, Can You Still Serve God With An Unclean Record? Rev. Milton has been preaching and teaching God's word for over fifty years. He is thankful to share these encouraging words of his experiences in his first book helping others to know they can serve God no matter what their past, present or future life experiences have been, are or may be.

Rev. Jerome Milton was born in San Diego, California being orphaned as an infant, growing up in orphanages and foster care. After numerous foster care home disappointments, Rev. Milton found love and care from his foster mother who showed him he had great purpose in live. His mother always told him, "Jerome, don't let your abuse be your excuse."

Rev. Milton received a full athletic scholarship graduating with honors from UCLA. He earned his Master's of Ministry degree from Point Loma College. His Doctorate of Divinity was conferred by Easter Bible College.

Rev. Milton found his way to Texas, settling in Tyler where he is a highly acclaimed citizen. He was awarded the prestigious T. B. Butler award. He was instrumental bringing cultures together starting the annual Martin Luther King, Jr. Observation and March that continues in Tyler today. Rev. Milton was the "Pastor For The Day" delivering the opening prayer for the U.S. House of Representatives in 2012. In addition, Rev. Milton is recognized by Sports Illustrated Magazine for his track and field coaching winning ten straight championships.

Rev. Milton is the senior pastor of Open Door Bible Fellowship Church. Rev. Milton and his wife are devoted parents to their six adopted children.